Dad's Railroad

Dad's Railroad
The Mountain Goat

by Mary Patten Priestley
Illustrated by Jack Baggenstoss

PROCTOR'S HALL PRESS
SEWANEE, TENNESSEE

Copyright © 2012 by Mary Patten Priestley
Illustrations © by Jack Baggenstoss
All rights reserved

Published by
Proctor's Hall Press
P.O. Box 856
Sewanee, TN 37375

ISBN
978-0-9789768-8-0

Library of Congress Number
2012913971

Design by Latham Davis
Text in Adobe Jenson
Selected titles in Centaur

to our dads

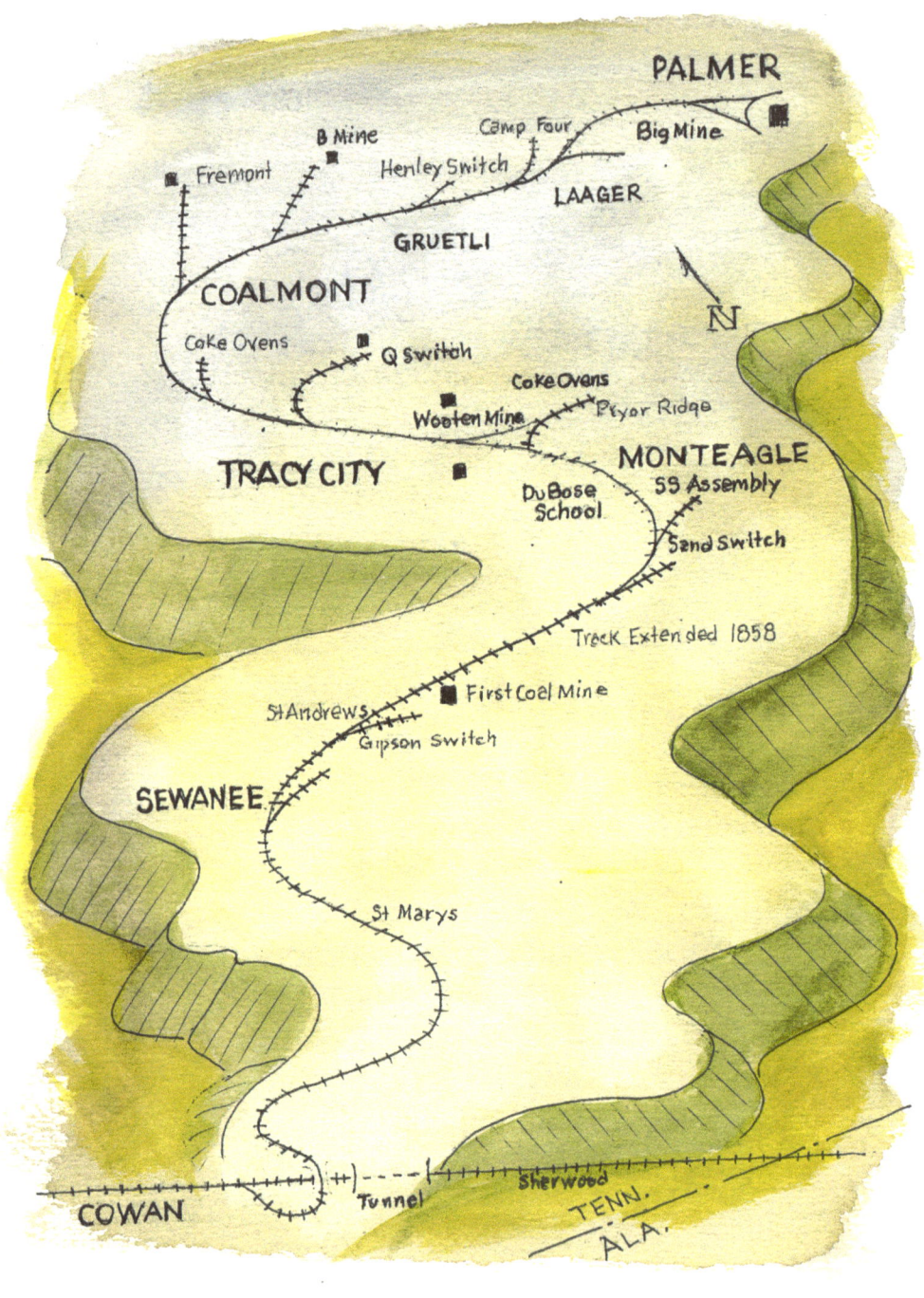

Preface

☾

The gift of a model train to the Grundy County Heritage Center by the late Cam Stewart, an ardent train buff, prompted Jack Baggenstoss to hatch the idea of this book. Working to develop the train set into a reproduction of the Mountain Goat railroad for the Heritage Center, Jack conceived of a children's book to accompany the model. A graphic artist, he suggested that he could do the illustrations if I would write the story.

I learned that as a boy Homer Kunz, whose father worked for the Mountain Goat, sometimes used his free pass to ride the train from Tracy City to Cowan to treat himself to an ice cream cone. In the summertime, he would pick blackberries from the train as it made its way slowly back up the mountain. That image was the germ of this story.

Dad's Railroad, the Mountain Goat is the tale of the short line railroad that first climbed the Cumberland Plateau above Cowan, Tennessee, in 1856, eventually connecting Cowan to Sewanee, Monteagle, Tracy City, Coalmont, and Palmer. It is told by 10-year-old Fritz, whose father is a brakeman on the Mountain Goat. He and the other children in the story represent the boys and girls who grew up around the Mountain Goat in the 1920s.

In *Dad's Railroad*, which takes place in the heyday of the Mountain Goat, Fritz's dad suggests that the railroad put the mountain on the map by bringing people up and transporting raw materials out to the rest of the South. Today, the Mountain Goat railroad is experiencing a rebirth as the Mountain Goat Trail, initiated by high school student Ian Prunty and carried on by the Mountain Goat Trail Alliance, local city governments, and others. It is the hope of many, including this author, that the Mountain Goat Trail will play a key role in the emergence of this mountain as a destination for sustainable recreation and the enjoyment of its natural beauty.

Thanks go to those who shared sites and stories, checked facts and grammar, corrected misconceptions, critiqued images, arranged for interviews, and generally helped us stay on the right track. They include Wanda and Lanny Bell, Carl Goodman, Oliver Jervis and the Grundy County Heritage Center, Cowan Railroad Museum curator Tom Knowles, Homer Kunz, John Kunz, Louise Geary Layne, Kimberly McBee, Nicole Nunley, Grady Ward Partin, Lynn Patten, Palmer historian David Patton, and Grundy County historian William Ray Turner. Book designer Latham Davis's ideas were just the ticket for transforming our somewhat nebulous plans into this very tangible book. *Grundy County* by James L. Nicholson and *The Mountain Goat* by J. W. Arbuckle and Alan C. Shook were invaluable resources. And Jack and I are most grateful for our traveling companions Hope Baggenstoss and Mac Priestley with whom chugging along is a great pleasure. All aboard!

MPP
August 2012

Shhh... Listen up...

Do you hear that long, low whistle off in the distance...?

That's the Mountain Goat train headed home to Tracy for the night. I'd say it's just topped the mountain, making its way through Sewanee. It's still a good ways from the Gizzard, maybe an hour off from here.

Some people say a train whistle's a lonesome sound. Not me! My dad's on that train. He's a brakeman, and that Mountain Goat is our bread and butter.

Every evening, that last train comes through, pulling empty coal cars back up from Cowan. Dad always leans out of the caboose and waves up at our house as he rides by. They leave the cars in the switchyard and pull the locomotive into the roundhouse for the night. Then my dad walks the tracks back home for supper. If it's after dark, all we can see of him is his kerosene lantern swinging by his side. We throw the door wide, and he grabs Ernst and me in a bear hug. Mama declares he's a sight for sore eyes.

My Mountain Home

~

Howdy! My name's Fritz, and today—July 1, 1923—is my birthday. I'm 10.

We live in Tracy City, the headquarters for the short line railroad that runs up the mountain from Cowan, through here, and clear out to Palmer. It's 40 miles long—not so "short" if you ask me—and plenty steep on the mountainside.

Dad's an air brake specialist. That's how we came to live here. Operating the brakes just right to get the Mountain Goat safely down the mountain takes experience and know-how. My dad's got both.

Before he was called in to help, they were having trouble with trains running away on the side of the mountain. Those trains carry heavy loads of coal, lumber, and sand.

    If the air brakes aren't handled right, the engineer can lose control and have a runaway. People get hurt, and freight gets dumped all down the side of the mountain.

Dad tried a lot of things to solve the brake problem. On one of his trial runs they left out down the mountain on a train loaded with all they could haul. It was too much. It got out of control—one great big hunk of iron, fire, and steam flying down the mountain. The engineer tried to jump off, but Dad and the fireman grabbed him, and they all held on for their lives. They still don't quite know how they made it.

Excepting that bit of excitement, things perked along, and pretty soon Dad had figured out the problem with the air brakes. Just as quick, he found out he had really taken a shine to Tracy City. Our family is Swiss, and there are a lot of Swiss people here and out in the Colony at Gruetli. So when they tried to talk him and Mama into settling down here, it was already near about a done deal.

Now Dad's on the Mountain Goat crew. He helps ease the train down the mountain every day. He lights out of here early in the morning, headed for the stationhouse. He's all over the train when they're loading up and switching cars on and off the sidetracks. Then he usually rides in the caboose with the conductor. The engineer operates the steam locomotive that pulls the train. The fireman rides up there with him, shoveling coal under the boiler to keep the steam coming. It's a hard job, and sometimes one of the brakemen has to help shovel.

Besides the train crews, the railroad's got people working in the stationhouse scheduling freight pick-ups and keeping the switchyard sorted out. Then there are the section crews. They take care of the track, which is no small task. It's uneven in a good many places, and that's where the cars tend to slip off the tracks. Derailments happen a lot, so the engine carries gear that the train crew uses to get the cars back on the rails. Dad says that's all in a day's work. Now if there's an emergency, like freight cars turned over, they have to get special equipment down from Nashville to handle it.

Tracy is right rough, kind of like a frontier town. It's close to 50 years old, but Dad says that's young for a town. When I was born, we lived in Dutch Town, the Swiss part of Tracy near the Henry Flury Store and just up from the stationhouse. But then Dad built this house up on the hill above the tracks.

Our home place is kind of in the woods. Mama keeps her loaded shotgun by the kitchen door. Any noise outside, and she grabs the gun. We don't have trouble with people stealing because she'd sprinkle their behind if she caught them.

My brother Ernst and I go to Shook School. I'm in fifth grade; he's in third. After school we've got night work at home: feeding the hogs and cattle, milking the cows, splitting and bringing in firewood, and carrying water.

We've got three cows and sell milk to two or three families, depending. We boys deliver milk in the afternoons. We carry it in covered lard buckets. Once I was lugging a lot of empty buckets home after dark. The only way I knew I was in the road was by feeling it sandy under my bare feet. I declare if I didn't plow right into a cow that was sleeping in the middle of the road! She went plumb crazy, started bawling, and the milk buckets scattered everywhere. I was on the ground an hour looking for those fool buckets.

Those cows, they're everywhere. We've got an open range law, and people run their cattle all over the mountain. The railroad has to pay for any that get hit by a train, so the crews spend an awful lot of time shooing those animals off the tracks.

Saturdays if we're caught up with our work Ernst and I play with the kids in Dutch Town. In the summertime we play ball. Our team—named Dutch Town—is half girls, but that's okay. The famous baseball pitcher Phil Douglas lives here. His two girls are on our team. We play against other teams, like Hoot and Gum Springs. We play some, get in an argument, fight, make up, and play some more.

The railroad runs through the middle of town. When the trains come by, the engineers throw gum to us kids. Sometimes if you've got a penny to spare, you can scamper up to the tracks, lay it down, and the train'll mash it even flatter than it was.

The stationhouse has trains coming in and out all day. They've got passenger and freight trains running down to Cowan and back four times a day and one out to Palmer. Those trains have to stay on schedule. Here's how to tell a railroad man: he's always pulling out his pocket watch to check the time.

They put the highway through here last summer, and it runs past our house. Ernst and I went up to watch the men driving steel to make dynamite holes for blasting. One of them asked where they could get drinking water. They hired my brother on right there for 15 cents an hour to take it to them. He'd jingle that money in his dadgum pocket like he was John D. Rockefeller.

Most roads around here are dirt . . . mud when it rains. So most everybody walks the railroad tracks to the store, to church, anywhere when they can. There's someone on the railroad all the time. You have to watch out, though, so you don't find yourself in a deep cut when a train is coming. Then you've got to high tail it out of the way or you sure enough could get run over.

Coal Country

We live in coal country. Back before the War Between the States, our mountain was covered for the most part with trees, with a clearing for a farm here and there. A man by the name of Wooten, looking for a groundhog that was eating his corn crop, was digging out its burrow under a sourwood tree. He scratched up what looked like rich dirt but turned out to be coal.

Word got around. Samuel Tracy, a man of some means, came down from New York, bought up a heap of land, and started the Sewanee Mining Company. He built the railroad from Cowan up the mountain to Lower Coal Bank, near what is now St. Andrew's, to haul coal down the mountain to the main railroad line.

It took a sight of money and a lot of men to lay that track all the way up this mountain. Watching the railroad work its way back and forth up the rocky slope, somebody called it the Goat Road. Somebody else said Mountain Goat, and that name stuck.

By the time they got the tracks laid to Lower Coal Bank, Mr. Tracy already realized that there wasn't much coal there. So they pushed the railroad across the mountain to where Mr. Wooten had first stumbled on the coal. They named the place Tracy City and started really opening some mines.

But just as they commenced hauling the coal out of here, the country got into a terrible war the likes of which nobody could have predicted. At different times, both Yanks and Rebs attacked the railroad and tore up the tracks.

After the war, the coal company rebuilt the railroad, better and stronger than before. And they started putting in beehive coke ovens near the Heading and at Lone Rock, different places around town. Workers would load the ovens with coal and seal them up except for a little hole. They'd set the coal on fire. After burning for two, three days at high heat and with almost no air, the coal turns into coke. Coke burns powerful hot. They load it onto the trains and send it down the mountain for making iron and steel.

Coke production also brought a heap of misery to Tracy City. The coal company leased prisoners from the state penitentiary to mine coal and work the ovens. They cost the company hardly anything.

That riled the other miners something fierce, because it looked like the biggest piece of their work was being taken over by jailbirds. They broke into the stockade where the prisoners were locked up, pulled them out, and burned down the building. Then they marched the convicts to the train, locked them into boxcars, and ordered the engineer to take them back to Nashville.

That didn't set well at all with the coal company. They built a new stockade and hauled the prisoners back to work. But everybody was really steamed up. Even after they shipped the convicts off for good, there were a powerful lot of problems. They had to call the National Guard in here. They set up tents and camped until things finally settled down and the miners got a contract they thought they could live with.

Tracy City

In spite of it all, Tracy City is a first-class town. We've got all kinds of stores where you can buy anything, the Dixie Theater, even a skating rink. We bottle Coca-Cola right here, and make scythes for farmers all over the world. And for sweets and breads I expect the Dutch Maid Bakery beats any around. People who come here to visit can stay at the Tidman House Hotel or out on the Big Fiery Gizzard at the White Hotel. And all those businesses keep the railroad mighty busy, bringing and taking people and things up and down the mountain.

Here's something funny: we got telephones in Tracy before we had electricity. We only got electricity because the Werner Lumber Company, which has a generator, supplies it after quitting time to 11 pm every day.

The lumber company's whistle is everybody's timepiece. Somebody sets down on that thing at 7:00 in the morning, then again before and after lunch, and finally quitting time at 5:00. You can hear it plumb out to Coalmont.

It's been close to five years since the one and only time that whistle got off its schedule. On the morning of November 11, 1918, it started blasting at 5:30 in the morning and just wouldn't cut off. Pretty soon the school bell joined in, and the churches, too. Mama sent me to find what the ruckus was about. I ran home with the gladsome news that the Great War had ended and everybody was celebrating! We all went uptown. Somebody suggested a parade, so people brought out all kinds of conveyances—cars, buggies, and wagons. Some rode horses.

We paraded out to Coalmont. The mayor gave a speech. Folks hooted and jumped for joy. It was a day for the history books, and we sure did it up right.

Like anyplace I guess, Tracy has its share of people who've barely got two nickels to rub together. You can tell some of the miners' families have it really hard. Same goes for mill workers. Some of them rent houses that are built close to the lumber mill. We call it Red Row, because that's the color they painted the houses. The people who live down there are very poor. Their kids are always begging cornbread from Mama. Once one of them told her, "My mama wants to borrow your shoes to go to town." She couldn't let them have her shoes.

Sometimes after dark, the men folk who live on Red Row gather around the tracks. When a train pulling a load of coal is trying to make it up the grade headed toward the Summit, going slow, they'll be up on top of the cars throwing the coal off. Then they'll jump off, collect the coal from all over the tracks, and take it home in buckets for heating and cooking.

There are some more mill houses near where we live. We call them Who'd a' Thought It. They got that name because a fellow walking down the track one time saw it was all woods. The next year when he noticed there were these houses in place of the trees, he declared in amazement, "Who'd a' thought it?!" That was too good to let drop.

Once some of us guys found a set of train wheels that had been on a railroad hand car, small ones. We set them on a siding, nailed on some boards, and we had our own flatcar. It takes about ten of us to push it up Myers Hill. At the top, we jump on and ride all the way back to town. It's a sure-enough heap of work, but worth it!

Those flatcar rides don't hold a candle to a real train trip down the mountain. Every now and then I get to take one of those.

Mountain Goat Trip to Cowan

Did I happen to mention that it's my birthday? I'm finally 10. Mama's taking Ernst and me down the mountain on the train to get an ice cream cone. You can't get ice cream on the mountain, and every now and then we ride down and have us some.

Because Dad's a railroad man we have free passes to ride the train whenever we want.

There's a station at Tracy, but you can get on or off the train pretty near anywhere. We catch it right in front of our house. We step up to the track, wave to the engineer, and he stops the train. With no more than a "Much obliged!" we jump on board. When we want off, the conductor pulls a cord to signal the engineer to stop the train for us.

The train goes mighty slow out of Tracy, blowing black smoke and cinders, pulling the grade to the Summit. Once we cross the bridge over the Big Fiery Gizzard, the first stop is Haynes Station.

We call this Yellow Crossing, because the little platform, which is open on three sides, is painted yellow. Wait 'til we come back up from Cowan: there'll be a buggy from the White Hotel waiting here for the train. The hotel is about a mile from the station, on the edge of the Fiery Gizzard. They send a buggy every time a passenger train comes up the mountain, in case there are hotel guests on it.

The hotel is a long wooden building, stretching along the edge of the bluff. There's a chalybeate spring below the bluff. Below that a dance pavilion stretches out over the Gizzard. People come to the hotel because of the spring. They say the chalybeate water is good for you. The guests bathe in the water, play croquet, and dance out under the stars. Me, I'd rather play ball.

Once a week, old Mr. White pays a lady to bring the mail out to the hotel. She gives us kids a dime to ride in her buggy to keep her company 'cause she's a-feared of that lonesome road. It's like a tunnel through the woods. It can be pretty scary on a foggy day.

People have been coming up to enjoy the summers at Monteagle for years. At first, they called this Moffat Station, after the man who put it on the map. John Moffat started the Monteagle Sunday School Assembly. The Assembly is like a little village of beautiful cottages that lie empty in the winter and suddenly fill up and come to life when summer gets here. A lot of those families pack picnics and come over to swim at Haynes Hole and Sycamore Falls.

We roll right on past the Sand Cut. They quarry sand here, and freight trains carry it south to be made into glass bottles. Just down the line a piece, we hit the Judd Cut, and it's all downhill from here.

Gipson's Switch is near the Lower Coal Bank, where the rail line stopped when Mr. Tracy first brought it up the mountain. St. Andrew's, a school for mountain boys run by a group of Episcopal monks, is here. It's a working school—you work half a day and go to school the other half. And you pay what you can. Dad says I might get to go there when I'm older.

Next stop: University Place. This is the site of the great University of the South, built on land that Mr. Tracy gave them. Most people don't stop to think that if he had found enough coal here the university would be someplace else entirely. And probably not too many people know that the university's nickname—Sewanee—comes from a coal company!

They say that 5,000 people rode the Mountain Goat up for the laying of the university cornerstone. That's hard to believe! Anyway, it was surely a big event.

William Howard Taft, the President of the United States, actually visited Sewanee once. Mama and Dad still talk about it. Mr. Taft's military aide, Archie Butt, wanted the President to see his alma mater. They rode up on the Mountain Goat.

    A horse-drawn buggy was decorated and ready to take them to campus when Mr. Sam Werner drove in from Tracy City in the only car on the mountain. President Taft was a good-sized man. He got in the car, and it took him up the hill without a whimper. His aides rode in the buggy. The very next year, Mr. Butt went down on the great Titanic.

We ease out from the Sewanee depot. The air brakes on all the cars are charged up, and we start slowly down the mountain. Holding the train in control takes the whole crew working together. The Mountain Goat swings around a curve, and we can see out over Hawkins Cove. Whoo-ee! Feels like we're just hanging on the side of the mountain.

If you look hard, you can see where St. Mary's Landing was, back when the convent was located on the bluff just above here.

Directly, we pass between the tall rock walls at the Slope Wall Cut. Sometimes University boys come out here and climb up on the rocks to look down on the train passing by, smoke and sparks pouring out of the smokestack. A fine sight!

Then it's down, down the mountain and into Hawkins Cove. Passenger trains aren't as hard to keep in check as the big freight trains loaded with coal, but the crew has to work hard every time. There are places where the tracks are uneven. And besides being steep, the railroad's got some tight curves. Nobody wants a derailment—or a runaway train.

Near the bottom, the train passes over the main Nashville-to-Chattanooga line just as that line enters the Cumberland Mountain Tunnel. Close to half a mile long, at one time it was the longest tunnel in the world, and the fastest ever dug out. They called it an engineering marvel. It's still one humdinger of a tunnel.

We cross that trestle and take one more curve. As soon as we make the valley, the track straightens out. We can see the Cowan depot, and the engineer lays on the whistle to let 'em know we're coming.

Cowan is the railroad junction. When people need to go to Chattanooga or Nashville, they switch trains here. They can ride down from Tracy in the morning, go to the big city for the day, and get home that night.

As soon as the train pulls up to the depot, Ernst and I jump off. Elbowing each other something fierce, we race across to the Franklin House hotel. Mama, hurrying close behind, cautions us to stop being so feisty. The restaurant is usually full of traveling salesmen and others who are staying at the hotel. Passengers coming through or changing trains stop in and get a good meal, and the air is full of good smells.

But we're on a mission. They serve all three flavors of ice cream here. We order one cone each of chocolate and vanilla. I'm partial to chocolate, and Ernst likes vanilla. Mama always gets a dish of strawberry.

Ice cream doesn't last long on a hot day in July. That tasty treat starts melting before I even get my first good lick. You gotta work fast, or you'll end up with nothing but a sweet, sticky puddle. It's a mess, but sure is good!

We do around town awhile, taking in the sights. Before the afternoon is half passed we skedaddle back to the train for the ride home. The whistle blows, the fireman shovels coal into the boiler, the train gives a jolt, and we are off. Smoke pours out of the smokestack, and the train crawls slowly up the mountainside.

Mama lets me stand on the back platform and pick blackberries as the train trundles along. A fellow doesn't turn 10 every day.

The Search for More Coal

There are railroad lines running up all the hills around town—Clouse Hill, Pryor Ridge, Nunley Ridge, and Flat Branch—each one going to a different mine. But just about the time Dad and Mama moved to Tracy City, the mines here were starting to play out, and the company was on the lookout for more coal.

They pushed the railroad to Coalmont, where there's so much coal they can't hire enough miners to dig it. Things are different out there. The mines in town have names like Rattlesnake, Possum Tail, and Wildcat, or they are named for people. But out in Coalmont, they're just A Mine, B Mine, and so on. All business.

The town of Coalmont is pretty small. Besides the depot, there's the Wigwam Hotel and an Episcopal church, St. Alban's. The biggest building in town, though, has a lot going on: there's a post office and a bank downstairs, and upstairs is the company store. Sometimes summer people headed to the resort at Beersheba Springs ride the train this far and take a buggy on out to the resort.

Here's something this town can brag about: at Coalmont the train has to stop for the traffic, and not the other way around. It's one-of-a-kind in the whole USA. There's a blind curve at the crossing, so the railroad men decided just to pull the train to a stop instead of flying around the curve and chance running smack into somebody they can't see.

I was six when they finished the railroad line all the way to Palmer. They made fast work of it: there were four camps working on it at once, and — all business — they just numbered them: Camps One, Two, Three, and Four.

The coal company built Palmer from scratch, and it pretty near sprouted up overnight. It has a company store and a post office. A movie theater, too. They rent company houses to some of the miners and their families. They all shop at the company store.

People have followed the coal from Tracy to Coalmont and Palmer to work in the mines. When they opened the Palmer Big Mine, we had a big do. They put two extra passenger cars on at Tracy, and we all rode out there for the festivities. We had a ball.

That afternoon I ran into Louise, a girl who used to be in my class at Shook School. Her dad and big brothers are miners. They live in a company house in Palmer, and she's in school here.

Just like us, most kids in Palmer walk home for lunch, and a lot of them have to cross the tracks. We do it all the time. But one thing you never do is crawl under the cars or climb over the couplings that hook them together, because that's how you can really get hurt. And if they catch you doing it, you know for sure what's coming when you get home.

Well, Louise let me in on a secret. One day a couple of her friends, rushing home for lunch, got in a fix. A line of coal cars was strung all the way through town, blocking their way. Hungry and in a hurry, they decided to scoot under one of the cars to get across. It was scary, because any little push from the engine could have started the cars rolling right over those two. But they made it, and so far their mama hasn't found out about it.

Louise had a scare of her own. She almost got run over by a train. Her mama had sent her down to the company store late one evening to get nickel cakes for the men's lunch pails. Coming home, she dropped one on the tracks.

A train was coming. She was scared her mama would whip her for losing the cake, so she stopped to pick it up. I guess she didn't know any better. That huge locomotive was pretty near on her, and when they blew that train whistle it about scared her to death. Lucky she collected her wits and scurried out of the way in the nick of time.

I'd say she gave that engineer a fright, too.

From what I can tell, a coal miner's job is about the dirtiest and most dangerous there is. They're carted in to work all day way underground, digging and blasting out the coal in tunnels too low to stand up straight in. The ceilings are propped up with wood, which can collapse and you can have a cave in.

The miners wear blue jeans with kneepads sewn inside, and they hook carbide lamps to their caps so they can see to work. All day long they breathe that stale, dusty air. And sometimes the coal dust can even cause an explosion.

The miners pile the coal into carts and roll them out of the mines. Each mine has a tipple—a place where the coal is loaded into railroad cars. At the smaller mines, they just tip the carts and pour the coal in—that's how tipples got that name. But at the Palmer Big Mine the tipple is a big thing. Inside, workers separate the coal from rock and rubbish before dumping it into the coal cars.

Palmer has more coal than any of the other places along the line, and they say it's all high-grade. They are really shipping the coal, thousands of tons a day. Every day, in the late afternoon, there's a coal train out of Palmer, a great long thing, sometimes 35 cars long. People sitting on their porches can see the fireman shoveling coal as the train heads to Tracy.

Camp Four and the Swiss Colony

~

Just this side of Palmer the railroad passes through Henley's Switch. Then on back this way a piece it comes to Camp Four. Out here, the Werner Lumber Company has a narrow gauge dinky rail line that they use for their logging operation. A little steam engine pulls the dinky train all out in the Savage to pick up logs. At Camp Four they use a boom to load logs from the dinky cars into freight cars called gondolas for the trip on the main line to the lumber mill in Tracy City.

I've gotten to ride the dinky train twice. Last time, the line went out as far as Meadow Branch. Now Mr. Werner's talking about running it way up around the side of Jumping Branch. Folks are all trying to tell him which a-way to build it, but he's not studying on taking their advice.

After the War Between the States, some families in Switzerland bought acreage for farming out here, sight unseen. When those people got here, they were bewildered to see that the land was all in forest, not farmland. Some went back, but most were obliged to stay, and more came on later.

They made good-sized clearings for farms and built houses. The Colony was officially founded in 1869. They named it Gruetli.

The Swiss Colony is a success, due in no small part to our Swiss ingenuity. The farmers raise beef cattle and dairy cows, make cheese, and grow vegetables. Some families keep bees and collect honey. They grow grapes, and many of them make their own wine. Some tend orchards and make cider using their own cider mills.

Many a Saturday, colonists ride the train into town and bring cheese and all kinds of garden produce to sell. Some of them have moved to Tracy City and started businesses.

A Good Place to Live

My dad's pretty smart. I guess you figured that. He says the coal brought the railroad here, but the railroad put this place on the map. More trains than ever are chugging down the mountain carrying coal to the steel mills, sand to the glass factories, and lumber all over the South. And more and more people are riding up to live and work, go to college, or escape the city life for a few days or weeks. I reckon Mr. Tracy would be amazed if he could see his Mountain Goat today!

They're fixing to hold the first Grundy County Fair in Summerfield next year. Word is they're going to judge animals, canned goods, baked goods—pretty near everything. It's a mite early, but I'm thinking about fattening up a hog to show. Dad wants Mama to enter her Damson preserves. I'm sure she'd win hands down.

Mama tells me I'm lucky to be growing up here on the mountain, playing with my Dutch Town friends, catching crawdads in the Gizzard, and every now and then taking a fancy to ride the Mountain Goat out to the Colony or down to Cowan.

Someday I'd like to catch the train to Nashville or Chicago—maybe even Florida. But I'd be sure-enough crazy to leave here for good. I'm proud to be living right here by Dad's railroad, and I reckon this is where I'll stay.

Mountain Goat Railroad Timeline

☾

1842 – Ben Wooten discovers coal in his cornfield in Tracy City

1845 – Nashville and Chattanooga Railroad is chartered

1852 – Samuel Tracy and other investors purchase land and incorporate the Sewanee Mining Company; the 2,228-foot Cumberland Mountain Tunnel is completed

1854 – Nashville and Chattanooga railroad is completed

1856 – The world's steepest railroad for its time (averaging a 3-percent grade), the Mountain Goat railroad is completed to Lower Coal Bank and the first coal shipment made; railroad is immediately extended toward Tracy City

1857 – A party from Beersheba Springs surveys a location near the Lower Coal Bank where Samuel Tracy has offered to donate 5,000 acres for a new university

1858 – First shipment of coal is made from Wooten No.1 mine in Tracy City

1859 – Southern bishops of the Protestant Episcopal Church meet at Beersheba Springs to draw up a charter for The University of the South

1860 – Sewanee Mining Company is reorganized as the Tennessee Coal and Railroad Company; the cornerstone of The University of the South is laid

1861-1865 – The Civil War (War Between the States)

1866 – Railroad is rebuilt; coal mining resumes

1868 – The University of the South opens; Captain Eugen Plumacher, representing the Swiss Emigration Society, considers establishing a Swiss colony on the mountain. Peter Staub purchases 15,000 acres and advertises it in Switzerland

1869 – First Swiss colonists arrive, and the colony, named Gruetli, is established

1870 – John Moffat purchases land and moves to what will become Monteagle

1873 – Fairmount Female College is founded in what will become Monteagle; coke ovens are constructed near the heading in Tracy City and tended by convict labor; Fiery Gizzard iron furnace is built, functions for three days proving that iron can be smelted using Sewanee coke; Nashville and Chattanooga Railroad is reincorporated as Nashville Chattanooga and St. Louis Railway (NC&StL)

1882 – Tennessee Coal and Railroad Company becomes Tennessee Coal, Iron, and Railroad Company (TCI); Monteagle Sunday School Assembly is incorporated

1883 – Coke ovens constructed at Lone Rock, tended by convict labor

1887 – Nashville, Chattanooga, and St. Louis Railway (NC&StL) purchases the Mountain Goat short line railroad from TCI

1892 – Free miners storm the stockade at Lone Rock in Tracy City, burn it down, and send the convicts back to Nashville on the train

1893 – Air brakes are adopted as standard equipment on U.S. trains

1896 – Convicts are removed from Tracy City permanently

1904 – National Guard is called in to Tracy City because of violence between union and nonunion miners; railroad tracks are laid to Coalmont

1905 – Tennessee Consolidated Coal Company (TCC) buys the former TCI

1914-1918 – World War I (the Great War), which increases the demand for coal

1917 – Fairmount Female College closes; railroad to Palmer is completed

1918 – Coal is first mined at Palmer

1922 – Dixie Highway constructed; U.S. demand for coal decreases and does not pick up until 1939

1924 – First Grundy County Fair is held in Summerfield

1920s and early 1930s – NC&StL railway company operates buses from Tracy City to Cowan to replace some of the passenger trains that are more expensive to run

1929 – New York stock market crashes

1935 – Arsonist burns much of Tracy City's business district

1936 – Werner Lumber Company closes

1930s – Late in the decade passenger service to Palmer is discontinued

1939-1945 – World War II, which increases the demand for coal through the 1950s

1940s – NC&StL begins replacing steam locomotives with diesel

1957 – NC&StL merges with Louisville and Nashville Railroad (L&N); strip mining begins in Grundy County

1962 – Interstate 24 north of Monteagle opens

1967 – After several years of violence and property destruction, TCC closes its mining operation in Palmer

1971 – Last passenger train from Cowan to Tracy City; Seaboard Coast Line Railroad purchases L&N

1970s – Arson destroys several buildings in Tracy City, including the train depot (1971), Tennessee Consolidated Coal Company office, Shook School, and Dixie Theater

1977 – Mountain Goat runs are switched to nighttime so locomotives can be used on the main line during the day

1985 – Rail service on the Mountain Goat ceases, and the rails are taken up

1986 – Seaboard and Chessie System, Inc. merge to form CSX Transportation

About the Author

Mary Patten Priestley grew up on Lookout Mountain, came to Sewanee for college, and put down roots here. She is curator of the Sewanee Herbarium and editor of the herbarium's quarterly newsletter, the *Sewanee Plant Press*. She wrote *Hike 'Em All at South Cumberland* and co-authored and illustrated *Go Take a Hike*, a guide to hiking on the Domain of the University of the South. Mary is a regular contributor to *The Tennessee Conservationist*, which is the magazine of the Tennessee Department of Environment and Conservation, as well as to the Friends of South Cumberland's quarterly newsletter. A member of the Tennessee Native Plant Society, she has served as the society's president and assisted in writing and editing the TNPS field guide, *Wildflowers of Tennessee, the Ohio Valley, and the Southern Appalachians*. *Dad's Railroad* is her second children's book. The first, *William's Wildflowers*, is a guide to wildflowers of the Southern Appalachians. Mary is leader and accordion player for the Bazzania Girls' Band. She and her husband Mac are the parents of three grown children.

About the Illustrator

Jack Baggenstoss attended Shook School, St. Andrews, and Grundy County High. He finished college at Tennessee Tech. After a tour of duty in the Navy, he began his career as an illustrator in Huntsville, Alabama, working as a sketch artist producing conceptual illustrations for future space vehicles and missions. He later moved his family to Montgomery, Alabama, and became the art director for a book publishing firm. While in Montgomery, he founded a graphic arts company, producing materials for area publications. After 20 years in Alabama, Jack returned to the mountain and spent the next 18 years as a regional sales representative for a large Birmingham printer. For the last several years he has been the "local guide" for a plein air group of artists from Atlanta. Presently, his main focus is landscape watercolor painting. Jack and Hope have two grown children.

www.ingramcontent.com/pod-product-compliance
Lightning Source LLC
Chambersburg PA
CBHW060755090426
42736CB00002B/45